Humans

# HUMANS

Tara J. Gonzales, M.A.

Copyright © 2015 Tara J. Gonzales

All rights reserved. No part of this publication may be reproduced, distributed, or transmitted in any form or by any means, including photocopying, recording, or other electronic or mechanical methods, without the prior written permission of the publisher.

Published by:
Sassaphrass Publications
Coppell, Texas 75019

ISBN: 0997374306
ISBN-13: 9780997374308

*Special thanks to Christopher R. Molina, and Adonica J. Guerrero, for helping to turn my dreams into realities.*

~

Humans

# DEDICATION

This book is dedicated to my grandmother, Beatrice, and to my mother, Olean. Thank you both for teaching me to always look people in the eyes, and to know that human equality varies only to the degree by which their actions speak.

Humans

# ACKNOWLEDGMENTS

I would like to thank Dr. Linda Montgomery and Dr. Sherry McKibben for introducing me to the world of scientific research, and for giving me the opportunity to present alongside other professionals in my field.

.

Dr. Jacobs, Dr. Olsen, Dr. Harter, and Dr. Thompson…thank you, for fostering my love of research and for being the greatest professors, and mentors, a student could ever have the pleasure of knowing. I will carry the knowledge attained under your direction, for the rest of my professional career.

I feel extremely fortunate to have had the opportunity to work with each and every single one of you!

There are approximately

Over

7 billion people

300 million

living on earth....

in the U.S.

Slavery is
illegal in
every
country…

...all law abiding

citizens are

ZERO awarded

living

the same

traditional

basic

slaves...

rights...

in the

United States

of

America…

...yet,
 racial inequalities are still the primary sources of animosity between 'Black', 'White', and 'Asian' American citizens.

Why???

## Fact:
# You are all human...

You all have the same basic needs...

Eat

Sleep

Survive

You all have to share this earth... Like it, Or Not....

so, now what?

Humans

# CONTENTS

| | |
|---|---|
| Preface: How it Began | 1 |
| Chapter 1: The Issues | 9 |
| Chapter 2: Human Division | 17 |
| Chapter 3: Human Enslavement | 25 |
| Chapter 4: The Solution | 31 |
| Chapter 5: The Study | 39 |
| Abstract | 45 |
| Chapter I: Introduction | 47 |
| Chapter II: Methods | 62 |
| Chapter III: Results | 67 |
| Chapter IV: Discussion | 84 |
| References | 97 |

# Preface: How it Began

Topics of discussion regarding race and ethnicity continue to feed socio-cultural tensions. While scientists have strived for centuries to understand racial differences, in order to understand a variety of behavioral and medical conditions, one cannot ignore the fact that race does not guarantee in-group homogeneity.

Why? People are shaped by a variety of variables, from biology to personal experience. Although race can certainly act as a commonality between two people, many times it is the only similarity. For that reason, it is only logical that not all people of a certain race have the exact same values, opinions, moral code, and so forth. This is why one cannot conclusively state that all Whites like a certain food, or that all Blacks have a certain fear, etc., without sounding irrational. For, when studying humans there are always exceptions.

When trying to understand people, one should be careful not to underestimate the importance of self-perception and self-identification as factors that help shape a person's identity. Identity is one of the prime factors that create socio-cultural differences between people belonging to the same racial group. So, why place so much emphasis on the variable of race itself?

In order to explain the importance of this book, I would like to share the personal experiences which prompted my desire to delve further into multicultural studies.

Racially, I am White. Ethnically, I am of a Spanish, Irish, and French ancestral mix. I was born in the United States of America. Both my parents, maternal & paternal grandparents, and maternal & paternal great grandparents, were born in the United States of America.

As a child, the primary language spoken in my home was English. As such, my primary language is English. Having taken Spanish as an elective in high school, my Spanish-speaking fluency level is fair. However, I am fluent in Spanish reading and writing.

I was raised by my mother in a single-parent, Christian home. She was raised with both parents in a matriarch headed family, with non-traditional gender roles. My father was also raised in a matriarchal structured family. As such, matriarch headed families and egalitarian interpersonal relationships are the only models to which I am accustomed.

It is the aforementioned variables, along with my personal experiences, that have helped shape both my personal and social identity...as well as how I view myself and how I carry myself in social settings.

Education was a high priority in my family. Both my parents have college degrees and there was never a doubt that I too would attend college, in hopes of one day earning my PhD. It was during the beginning of this particular educational journey that I was introduced to an overwhelming inconsistency between what I expected of myself, and what professors and fellow students expected of me.

While transferring from community college to a four-year university I encountered an advisor who refused to sign my degree plan, which was declaring psychology as my major and sociology as my minor. His stated reason being that he did not know me well enough to say I would be a good fit for the field of psychology.

He asked me if I had considered social work as a major and Spanish as a minor. Perplexed by what, other than my last name, would prompt such a suggestion, I asked him to please review my transcript so he would see that I was already working steadily toward attaining my psychology degree, and toward my goal of becoming a professor.

I had declared my major two years prior and was transferring with a 4.0 in my psychology coursework, along with recognition in a published textbook for aiding in the construction of an undergraduate clinical psychology course, and the corresponding manual. However, he refused. He told me to reconsider all of my options.

I informed him that social work was not an interest of mine, and that a Spanish minor would only be as beneficial to me as it would be to any student who was interested in fostering the understanding of a second language, which I was not. I was curious as to whether he was advising all students, Anglo, Black, and Asian, alike, to consider a Spanish minor, but that is a curiosity that went unanswered. I reiterated that I preferred to major in psychology and minor in my initial stated field of sociology.

I explained that my mother also had a degree in psychology from the same university, and that I had been attending courses at the same university since I was a child, in hopes of following in my mother's footsteps. Still, he refused. So, I did the logical thing …found another professor to sign my degree plan, and continued on my initial path towards earning my degree in psychology.

It wasn't long after, while sitting in a gender studies course, that a professor asked our opinions on the importance of education. I shared my belief that education should be of the utmost importance…to which she replied, "That's interesting, considering that education among women in your culture is not very common….they're usually more concerned with having children and catering to their men in the kitchen."

Without thought, I retorted by questioning when the American culture had regressed. She then explained that she was referring to my "Mexican culture". I explained to her that not only was I American, my Hispanic ancestry originated in Spain, not Mexico. She replied with the comment, "Oh, it's all the same." Being the only Hispanic in the course, I had no one among me to help validate that she was greatly mistaken.

Instances of this nature continued throughout the duration of my undergraduate and graduate studies. While some might initially assume these individuals were racists, I believe that they were truly oblivious to their extreme multicultural ignorance. However, to merely blame their ignorance on their lack of exposure to other cultures would be irresponsible, as their professions demand multicultural awareness.

Therefore, I took it upon myself to delve into current multicultural studies, with hopes of having research to support my own truths. Unfortunately, the more I searched for information explaining that not all people of the same race are the same, the more I found studies that aimed at finding the reverse.

I also began to see a connection between patterns of differences between variables, such as: religious affiliation, familial structure, socioeconomic status, education, geographical location, etc., with people's overall social identity, and how these variables appeared to be more indicative of a person's overall identity, than was one's particular race and/or ethnicity.

It was at this time that I enrolled in an independent study course to conduct an IRB (Institutional Review Board) approved study, under the direction of Dr. McKibben, in order to evaluate social identity and differences among Hispanics. I opted to study only Hispanics for several reasons, the main being the most obvious…I am of Hispanic descent. Therefore, I have personal experience dealing with differences, and even discrimination, among people with my shared ethnic label.

The second reason for selecting Hispanic participants was because not all Hispanics share the same race. In fact, Hispanics are one of the few ethnic groups whose members can be further divided by the three primary races: White, Black, and Asian, which means that skin tone and physical features greatly affect people's perception of various Hispanics, creating a range of differences in Hispanics' overall social experiences.

It is my hope that the following study can be expanded, and utilized to help understand humans as a whole…rather than as members of a different class, based solely on pigmentation.

# Chapter 1
# The Issues

Understanding human functionality has been scientists' primary goal since the beginning of time. However, it is easy to see that regardless of the amount of studies conducted, and regardless of similarity, humans are exceedingly divided. The question is why?

➢ What are humans?

➢ What causes human division?

➢ What is the solution?

These are all questions that require answering if humans truly want to peacefully coexist on this earth...as so many claim to want. If that is true, then it is no longer enough to merely state that you want peace. It is time for all humans to start making conscious choices to stop behaviors that help to maintain human division.

The excuse that 'nothing will ever change' is only a fact because generally speaking, most humans do not care enough to contribute to the change.

Later, I will discuss various theories regarding why humans not only want, but encourage, human division. But for now, I would like to discuss the one human divide to which we can all relate...race.

## What exactly is race?

Race is a socially constructed term used to classify people with shared physical traits, such as: skin tone, hair type, and shape/ position/size of various primary facial features, such as the eyes, nose, and mouth. Although the term race, in itself, seems like a harmless word...the negative implications behind its utilization have proven colossal. But, why?

Somewhere between the 15th and 17th centuries, scientists claimed to have discovered cranial differences between people sharing the previously mentioned physical features. They determined that human remains could be classified and identified as being of African (Negroid), European (Caucasoid), and Asian (Mongoloid) descent. However, although skeletal and other physical differences do seemingly exist...all humans, regardless of race, remain 99.9% genetically identical to one another.

The validity of this determination gives rise to a multitude of unanswered questions regarding the importance of distinctions between various humans.

➢ What is the importance of physical differences among humans?

➢ Why are so many humans determined to be the same?

➢ Why are so many humans afraid, indifferent, and/or un-accepting, of humans who look different than themselves?

➢ What will it take to stop racism among the human species?

While the majority of race studies tend to seek the differences between various races, I am interested in evaluating the similarities between racial and ethnic groups. Primarily because, even if there are physical differences between people from different regions, all still share the most basic classification…their species.

Regardless of ethnicity, all people are human. They all belong to the animal kingdom and are all primates. In fact, the manner in which we socialize, and our living environments, are the primary factors which separate humans from other mammals in the animal kingdom. To discriminate against another human based on race or ethnicity would be like a dog discriminating against another dog because of the color of the other dog's coat…irrational.

## Examples of Species Within The Animal Kingdom

| Human | Dog | Chimpanzee | Dolphin |
|---|---|---|---|
| **Kingdom:** Animalia  **Phylum:** Chordata  **Class:** Mammalia  **Order:** Primates  **Family:** Hominidae  **Genus:** Homo  **Species:** Sapiens | **Kingdom:** Animalia  **Phylum:** Chordata  **Class:** Mammalia  **Order:** Carnivora  **Family:** Canidae  **Genus:** Canis  **Species:** Familiaris | **Kingdom:** Animalia  **Phylum:** Chordata  **Class:** Mammalia  **Order:** Primates  **Family:** Hominidae  **Genus:** Pan  **Species:** Pan Troglolytes | **Kingdom:** Animalia  **Phylum:** Chordata  **Class:** Mammalia  **Order:** Cetacea  **Family:** Delphinidae  **Genus:** Stenela  **Species:** Stenella Longirostris |

So, if race is a socially constructed term, and people have obvious physical differences, where do the differences end…and do they outweigh the similarities?

The answer is both simple and complex. Think of race (Asian, Black, White) as you would think of the term 'breed' (e.g., terrier), and the term ethnicity (e.g., Chinese, African, Hispanic, etc.) as variety (e.g., jack Russell terrier, American Staffordshire Terrier, etc.), if you will. In dogs, for example, for every breed there are differences within the breed…including, but not limited to: coat, eye color, size, weight, class, and temperament.

The same is true for humans. For every race there are differences within these races…including, but not limited to: skin tone, eye color, size, weight, class, and temperament. Similarly, as with dogs, the most important social characteristic for any human would be their temperament/personality…if the goal is to ensure they are productive members of society.

Now, if it really is that straightforward, why do so many people place so much emphasis on race and ethnicity? And, why does discrimination continue to exist?

The answer is simple. We have been conditioned to believe that people who look different cannot be the same. Worse, we have been conditioned to believe that the less a person looks like us, the higher the likelihood that they are not as 'good' as we are. That is illogical. You are no more a good person, because of your physical appearance, than anyone else.

However, we have been conditioned to believe that a person's physical attributes will tell you what that person will be like. The problem is, while stereotypes are based on partial truth…if we delved deeper into the facets that fuel these stereotypes, which often lead to racist attitudes, we would find that there are more differences within individual racial and ethnic groups, than there are between the members of these groups.

In order to do that, let us discuss various groups….

# Chapter 2
## Human Division

Now that we've discussed the three primary, socially derived, races...Asian, Black, and White, let us discuss various racial subgroups, or ethnicities, in order to understand how these classifications relate to culture, social identification, and human division.

Among Asians, you have a variety of subgroups (ethnicities) including, but not limited to: Chinese, Mongolian, Korean, Indian, etc. Among Blacks, subgroups include, but are not limited to: Afro-Asiatic, Afro-Caribbean, Afro-American, Khoisan, etc. Among Whites, subgroups include, but are not limited to: Spanish, Italian, Irish, German, etc.

As you can see, ethnic groups are chiefly based on geographical location. Depending upon your personal beliefs, the reasoning for the similarities between people in different regions may vary. However, the simplest and most probable explanation is that people have a tendency to migrate towards, and with, people of shared likenesses. Therefore, it is highly likely that from the beginning of time, when people begin populating and exploring the world, they traveled with either family, or with those whom they had the most in common.

The more people explored, the more people were exposed to other humans; some with shared physical attributes, some completely different. Now, one cannot say for certain what caused people to develop racist attitudes towards those who did not share the same physical attributes. However, it may be fair to say that fear is the primary emotion behind racism. How so?

Few people would argue with the notion that their life would be perfect if they had a comfortable place to call home, plenty of food on the table, and at least one other person with whom to enjoy life…all without anyone negatively affecting them.

In fact, so many people have the same goal, that achieving that goal…in itself…has become a driving force in competitive industries, including: housing, retail, and employment. The more people in one region, the more difficult it is for everyone to earn the same amount of money…making housing, food, and clothing, commodities that are not evenly distributed among the population. People fear both not having a sufficient amount of resources, as well as having their resources taken away.

As the world's population increases, resources have a tendency to decrease. As previously mentioned, humans are a species who belong to the animal kingdom. As living beings, humans have certain innate instincts to survive. In order for humans to survive they require sustenance.

The introduction of the monetary system largely contributed to our current way of living. It is the strongest motive in countless crimes. However, in a monetary system, acquiring sustenance generally requires you to have money. In order to have money you typically must have a source of income. Although earning money can be achieved a variety of ways, given the population of the world, there is simply no way to ensure that everyone's needs will be met. As such, humans have developed a sense of competition.

As is true in other species, there are human alpha types. Correspondingly, there are humans who are less dominant. It is that initial sense of dominance that places humans on an uneven keel. It is the fear of being 'at the bottom of the barrel' that causes people to feel the need to either attain, and/or maintain, a perceived spot at the 'top'. As such, they begin searching for possible distinctions between one another, which might help them reach that goal. Because skin tone is the most visible distinction, it is often the first to be attacked.

It is said that a human's ability to produce and communicate rational thoughts, are what distinguishes humans from other 'less civilized' animals. However, if you take a look at history, along with the current state of the world, few could argue that we are much different than a pack of wild wolves. In fact, humans have proven to be far more violent and self-serving in nature than any other animal on the planet. The question is, can this be fixed? The honest answer is, no. Because, as with other animals, not every human is stable.

However, if all humans worked together with the common goal being for every human to have equal access to the luxuries of the world, then things could get better.

Given that racism is a global problem which has lead to the demise of so many humans…it is my personal belief that reducing racism can lead to a domino effect of positive change in this world. Therefore, the quickest way to create a cohesive society is to help people change any irrational race-related thoughts that they have been conditioned to believe. The most productive way to achieve this, is to show people that our differences are all socially created.

So, let us discuss some of these socially created differences. Socially created, referring to the areas in people's lives over which they have control, from religion to personal opinion, rather than areas in which they have no control, e.g. genetics, birthplace, etc.

Earlier I discussed how competition can lead to division. Now, I am going to assume that everyone reading this book is familiar with the terms slavery, inequality, and discrimination. Therefore, without delving into an in-depth history lesson on issues of human enslavement, let us just assume that it is common knowledge that slavery has existed, in every culture, from the beginning of time.

Sadly, humans are so competitive that they often feel the need to compare slavery between racial groups, in order to prove that people with their shared traits experienced a more difficult enslavement than others. They do this in order to rationalize holding onto racist ideation, rather than being equally upset with all human enslavement. Sounds ridiculous, does it not?

There is not a human on this earth who was able to control the level of pigmentation their skin would have at the time of their birth. Nor did they have any say in which country they were going to be born. They had no say what religion their parents were going to practice. Nor did they have any say into which type of governmental structure they were being born. Just as you did not have a say. Yet, these are the primary issues used to maintain human disagreements.

*"It is impossible to successfully move forward...*

*while staying in the past."*

One theory is that someone must be benefitting. But...

- ❖ Who?

- ❖ How does holding onto a fake notion regarding human inequality, based solely on skin tone, benefit anyone?

Well, generally speaking, humans want more. More of everything...from money to status. In order to get more one must produce more. From the beginning of time, those in power have used the less fortunate to achieve their ultimate goal...to 'have more'.

Human exploitation is common throughout history. Therefore, let us discuss the topic of human enslavement, in order to help shed some light on the benefits of racial division, and how the two work simultaneously to help maintain hierarchy among humans, whereas those at the top stay at the top.

Take a quick glimpse at history and you will discover that members of 'Asian,' 'Black,' and 'White' humans have all been enslaved, discriminated against, and/or maltreated, at some point in time. In fact, racism, sexism, and other types of discrimination continue to exist today.

There are approximately 7 billion people on earth, just over 300 million in the United States of America. Of those Americans, there is less than 1% chance that any of those people were ever traditional slaves, or children of a slave, here, in the United States of America. That is almost 300 million people, with absolutely no first-hand experience being a traditional slave. Moreover, although illegal human trafficking continues to exist across the world, slavery is illegal in every country. In addition, all law-abiding citizens of the United States of America, regardless of race, are awarded the same basic rights. Still, racial division continues. But, why?

Who keeps those animosities alive?

The answer is easy. You, and/or the people around you, do. Humans keep animosities created by generations past, alive in the present…by refusing to let go.

'Letting go' in this instance, is not meant to be synonymous with being uncaring for the humans who were enslaved, who have been treated inhumanely, or who have literally fought the fight against human division. Nor does it mean being ignorant to the fact that divisions continue to exist. Instead, it means letting go of the anger, the animosity, and the burden, that your ancestors lived and died over. You can recognize, understand, and even sympathize with their struggle, without mistaking their struggle, as your own. Or, without assuming that people, who resemble past slave owners and/or slaves, are to blame for every inconsistency in your life.

It is impossible to move forward while remaining in the past. There are opinions regarding discrimination, and then there are facts...

- ✓ You are all human.
- ✓ You all have the same basic needs.
- ✓ You all have to share this earth...

...so, now what?

Humans

# Chapter 4
## The Solution

It is said that in order to discover a solution to any problem, you must first admit that a problem exists. I can personally attest to the fact that a problem does exist. Regardless of your personal opinion regarding racism, discrimination against humans of all types exists. White, Black, and Asian humans all experience discrimination on a daily basis. It is irrational. It is inhumane. It is unnecessary. It needs to stop, if humans truly desire to live in a more peaceful environment.

Secondly, you must accept the role that you play in maintaining the problem. Admitting that you are part of a problem can be as difficult as making changes. Nevertheless, you must be willing to accept the possibility that the answer to your problem may not be consistent with your own previous personal opinions and/or likes.

Lastly, you must be willing to implement a solution by taking an active role in the change. Restating the past in order to justify the current state, is as helpful as not saying anything at all. Therefore, rather than restating what was and focusing on what is (because of what was), humans need to start focusing on what needs to be done…in order to guarantee that the future becomes what they want it to be. They need to take action.

If you want peace, you need to take action…even in matters as small as removing racial labels from your everyday speech, e.g., instead of stating, "a Black woman helped me", say, "a woman helped me...", or rather than, "a White man held the door open", say, 'a man held the door open'.

Why?

Because if people are all humans, the less racial distinctions we make in our personal lives, the less distinction we will see when socializing and interacting with humans who do not share similar physical appearances. And, although we have no control over other people's actions…if everyone reading this book makes an active change, then it is possible that enough humans can begin to create a universal change, for future generations.

While the sentiment may seem idealistic, one fact remains the same; inactivity is a form of acceptance. But, just as humans are taught how to add and subtract, they can be taught the proper way to treat one another.

So, if the goal is to coexist with minimal disruption, where might humans begin?

Well, as previously mentioned, it is irrational for humans to believe that they can successfully and peacefully coexist, while continuously bringing up the struggles of past ancestors. Unfortunately, humans are set on holding onto the past... not for the mere purpose of learning, but often, in order to use past prejudices to maintain current animosities between those who feel their ancestors were victimized, and those who believe their ancestors were the wrongdoers. This cycle has existed among humans for centuries.

But what would happen, let's say, if rather than devote lessons to Black slavery, in the United States, students were regularly taught the contributions of all cultures: Black, White, and Asian, alike? After all, is the U.S. not supposed to be a melting pot?

What if slavery was taught only to the extent that at one point in time various humans (Black, White, and Asian, alike) were inhumanely enslaved, and because of that, traditional slavery is no longer legal in the United States, or anywhere else in the world?

What if positive outcomes became our main focus? Period. No need for emphasis on one particular group's enslavement, but rather teach children that all human enslavement is wrong, and we should all be grateful that it is now illegal in our country.

What if everyone began to teach children that discrimination against other humans, for any reason, e.g., race, religion, sexuality, gender, age, intellect, is not just irrational, but also illegal?

What if we encourage all humans to report any discrimination they experience, and/or witness, rather than shame people or accuse them of playing the 'race card'?

Rather than focus on how awful it must have felt to be a Black person sitting in the back of the bus, we could teach future humans that at one point in time not all humans had equal rights, but that thankfully, because of humans like Rosa Parks, Martin Luther King Jr., etc., discrimination against humans is now illegal, and should be considered unacceptable under all circumstances, at all times, not only in the United States of America…but all over the world.

But let us not stop there. You might be thinking, 'we are already teaching our young those lessons.'

But, what are you actually doing?

At large, we are not following through with our own words. In fact, we are typically teaching students to frown upon segregation, while simultaneously segregating history into designated months, based on race. This not only sends a counterproductive message, it is an irrational means of creating racial cohesion.

The solution? Actually eliminate segregation across the board, no matter how subtle. For example, rather than designating months for specific racial groups, e.g., Black history month, Hispanic Heritage, etc., educate students about all human inventors, philosophers, and scholars. Treat Asian, Black, and White contributors equally, as a part of the overall general curriculum.

In addition, eradicate race-based criterion for admission and/or acceptance into any institution, association, club, school, etc. If humans are expected to be treated equally, then race should no longer be taken into consideration or asked of any candidate, for admission into anything…anymore…period. People are either humans, or they are not. They are either qualified, or they are not. Race should no longer be included on any application, nor should standards be altered on any standardized assessments and/or lists of qualifications, for applicants of different races.

As previously stated, at large, all humans posses the same basic needs: food, shelter, and clothing. There are Asian, Black, and White humans fortunate enough to be born with an abundance of resources. Conversely, there are people who will never know what it is like to have any resources…not because it isn't possible, but because that is just life.

There are poor Asian humans, there are rich Asian humans. There are poor Black humans, there are rich Black humans. There are poor White humans, there are rich White humans. Simply stated, there are poor humans and there are rich humans. Poverty has no race. It is up to each individual to educate themselves, in hopes that they will succeed in the only race we all have…the race to survive.

It should no longer be acceptable for humans to use race as a crutch, or as a stepping stone. It is up to all humans to make a positive difference if their goal is to live in a peaceful society, whereas all humans work collectively to make the world a more pleasant place to coexist.

Human success is possible regardless of the past and regardless of current racial divisions. There are nice humans; there are mean humans. There are intelligent humans; there are ignorant humans. There are good humans; there are bad humans…and so on.

Therefore, if humans truly wish to eliminate racism, they need to stop placing any emphasis on race. Period. Even in instances where they may benefit. Because, I repeat…humans are humans, and inequalities are more than skin deep.

So, now that we've discussed basic human labels, let us discuss what shapes humans…

# Chapter 5
## The Study

The manner in which a person acts and thinks, their likes and dislikes, etc., are all aspects that help make each person unique. Not only does this uniqueness mold an individual's personal identity, it also helps others distinguish individuals from members of a larger group. This holds true for people of all races and ethnicities. Therefore, assumptions regarding a person's identity, based solely on skin tone, are illogical. Rational beings know there are many differences among all people, even those with shared race and ethnicity.

As previously mentioned, a person is shaped by many variables, including, but not limited to: environmental factors, socioeconomic status, level of education, religiosity, familial structure, etc. Therefore, not all people of the same race identify with the same subculture(s). Subculture, in this instance, referring to the various groups that share similar interests and/or beliefs, taking into account factors like geographic location, religiosity, political affiliation, occupation, etc., as these elements influence a person's overall social identity.

Still, the question remains…given the fact that race alone cannot define an individual's identity, why does race continue to be considered a primary indicator in various studies? Why do scientists, and others, feel the need to make distinctions between race? While it is impossible to definitively answer those questions, race-based studies are abundant and many people believe that these studies help to feed discriminatory stereotypes that are attached to various racial groups…and they very well may have a point.

How can our society successfully create an overall sense of racial equality, if we continue searching for racial distinctions? Is it possible that we are underestimating the impact of predictive variables, relating to all living people, that can impact a person's character, e.g., the type of neighborhood in which one was raised, religious and/or political affiliations, familial structure, parenting styles, etc.? Is it possible that, if we looked beyond the race variable, we would discover more differences within races, than between races? Further suggesting that we all belong to the same race…the human race. Similar skin tones and distinctive physical features only shape a person's social identity to the extent that society expects of, and/or reacts to, individuals of various races…creating a variety of societal subcultures, which ultimately shapes a person's overall social identity.

These are issues that I have personally found intriguing for some time now. This interest intensified during the completion of graduate school, primarily because of the inconsistencies between how professors, textbooks, and other people perceived people of Hispanic ethnicity, and the overwhelming contradiction with all that I knew, as someone of Hispanic ethnicity.

In order to gain better perspective on these inconsistencies, I decided to take the scientific approach and conduct a research study. I began by conducting a preliminary study on Hispanic Social Identity in order to identify possible differences between Hispanics.

As hypothesized, results of the preliminary study showed distinct differences between Hispanic subcultures (some results with a standard deviation of zero), indicating a need for further examination. So, I conducted a second study using a second group of participants.

The following section is a copy of the study.

# Implications of Socio-Cultural Expectations on Identity:

# An Examination of American Born Hispanics

Abstract

Many mental health professionals strive to attain greater understanding of multiculturalism. A common assumption that all Hispanics share cultural beliefs exists among psychologists, and other fields alike, which can create contradictions between the expectations of how Hispanics should behave. The following research aimed to clarify that not all Hispanics possess common cultural attitudes, and/or customs, simply based on ethnicity. The purpose of this study was to examine the variations of social identity, within the Hispanic ethnic group, differentiating between those who identify more with American culture vs. those who identify with their Hispanic Culture, and how these variations correlate with the expectations of what defines Hispanic Social Identity. Results from an ANOVA and Pearson

Correlation, supported the hypothesis that $H_1$: A Hispanic's social identity would influence expectations of which culture other Hispanics "should" identify with, which would lead to prejudices within the Hispanic ethnic group.

# Chapter I

*Introduction*

Social and Cultural Expectations of American Born Hispanics: Examining Hispanic Social Identity and Socio-cultural Implications.

## Identity & Multiculturalism

Many researchers agree that identity development is a crucial component related to a person's overall well-being, not only in relation to self-esteem, self-efficacy, and self-concept, but also in regard to the prevalence and/or absence of a variety of mental disorders (Branscombe & Wann, 1994; Ethier & Deaux, 1994; Kiang, Yip, & Fuligni, 2008; Lannegrand-Willems & Bosma, 2006; McGinly et al., 2010; Njus & Johnson, 2008; Rotheram-Borus, 1990; White, Obrien, Jackson, Havalchak, Phillips, Thomas,

& Cabrera, 2008). Identity is a circular concept that may not only affect, but may also be effected by, a variety of personal life choices, e.g., whether or not to go to college, what morals and values to adopt, what style of clothes to wear, etc., and is often the result of a person's primary and secondary social groups, including culture (Hunter, Kypri, Stokell, Boyes, O'Brien, & McMenamin, 2004). Identity formation is highly complex and often times even more so among ethnic minorities who are faced with developing an identity in a racially biased society (Negy, Shreve, Jensen, & Uddin, 2003).

While it is not uncommon for non-minority individuals to classify minorities as one large group based on commonalities such as race, skin color, and geographical location, it is important to acknowledge that people belonging to the same racial group may have completely different social and/or ethnic identities (Huddy & Virtanen, 1995). This means that people's social and ethnic identities are not biologically based. Rather, social identity constructs are chosen and are largely dependent on non-biological factors that will determine and enhance one's personal expression of who they are and who they will choose to become (Ethier & Deaux, 1994; Markus, 2008). Therefore, it seems essential to note that researchers have found that social identity tends to be based more on the environmental and social inferences that compliment a persons' view of oneself, as well as how a person wishes to be viewed by others, rather than by one's race and/or ethnicity (Barlow, Taylor, & Lambert, 2000; Ethier & Deaux, 1994; Linton, 2004; Park-Taylor, Ng, Ventura, Kang,

Morris, Gilbert, Srivastava, & Androsiglio, 2008). Racially based assumptions can be detrimental to therapeutic success (Gurung & Mehta, 2001), and the impact of racial stereotypes and biases on the client-clinician relationship has been a topic of interest for many (Gurung & Mehta, 2001; Negy et al., 2003; Sue, Arredondo, & McDavis, 1992); primarily because most people would rather be judged on characteristics that they have control over, e.g. likes, dislikes, morals, and/or values, rather than on ascribed attributes that they have no control over, e.g. race/ethnicity, skin tone, and/or place of birth (Markus, 2008; Negy et al., 2003).

As diversity in the United States continues to increase, mental health professionals strive to attain greater understanding of multiculturalism (Basow,

Lilley, Bookwala, & McGillicuddy-DeLisi, 2008; Gurung & Mehta, 2001; Negy et al., 2003; Rotheram-Borus, 1990; Utsey, Chae, Brown, & Kelly, 2002). Most clinicians would agree that client-clinician coupling is crucial to a successful therapeutic relationship. The rise of culturally diverse client-clinician coupling has created an increased necessity for cultural awareness, in order to avoid misdiagnosis due to under/overestimation of stereotypic ethnic incongruencies (Gurung & Mehta, 2001). When becoming culturally aware, it is imperative for therapists to recognize the role of social and ethnic identity, and how the development of social identity correlates with overall quality of life and well-being (Basow et al., 2008; Gurung & Mehta, 2001; Negy et al., 2003; Rotheram-Borus, 1990; Utsey et al., 2002). A lack of cultural awareness can damage the client-clinician relationship. Therefore, in order to successfully provide a client with direction, it is crucial for therapists to be aware of how their personal experiences and biases can both facilitate and/or hinder their client's progress (Ford, 2006).

One important aspect of cultural awareness is an understanding that ethnicity does not necessarily define culture and/or social identification (Ford, 2006). Conflicting contexts between one's actual identification and their expected identification can cause undue stress, and it is not uncommon for ethnic minorities to feel additional pressure to address inconsistent cultural beliefs between their minority status and their level of identification with either the minority or the majority culture. This type of stress is referred to as acculturative stress (McGinley et al., 2010), and is increasingly evident among minorities in the United States who identify closely with their American culture, rather than the culture of their ancestors (Ethier & Deaux, 1994; Rotheram-Borus, 1990; McGinley, Carlo, Crockett, Raffaelli, Torres-Stone, & Iturbide, 2010).

## Identity & In-Group vs Out-Group

Prior research on the out-group homogeneity effect has indicated that people are more prone to recognizing differences between people not belonging to their own group (Branscombe & Wann, 1994; Lannegrand-Willems & Bosma, 2006; White et al., 2008). Group affiliation is one means of enhancement and/or maintenance of one's social identity, and social identity proponents assert that a person's level of contentment with their social identity will be largely based on in-group and out-group differentiation (DeCremer, 2001; DeCremer, VanVugt, & Sharp, 1999). Mental health professionals' understanding of social and ethnic identities is important, in this respect, primarily because a person's collective identity can affect their overall perception of other members of society, and may also determine the extent to which one interacts with and perceives members from other groups that they deem as dissimilar to their own (Ethier & Deaux, 1994; Huddy & Virtanen, 1995; Negy et al., 2003; Rotheram-Borus, 1990). Recognition of ones' own classification in relation to other people, who share common linguistic, educational, and other socioeconomical characteristics, is an important aspect of social identification, self-recognition, and self-acceptance (Ethier & Deaux, 1994; Linton, 2004). Therefore, some people feel that it is important for minorities to maintain close identification with their ancestral heritage (Linton, 2004). However, research suggests that people living in the United States, who identify themselves primarily as American, often have a greater sense of self efficacy than those who identify more closely with another nationality. On the other hand, people who place emphasis on their minority status, have a tendency to report higher feelings of inadequacy, than people who disregard their minority status. Similarly, people who identified themselves primarily as a minority reported feeling like they had fewer socioeconomic opportunities than the majority, as well as those identified more closely with the majority (Barlow et al., 2000). Similarly, Negy et al.

(2002) found that among White, Black, Asian, and Hispanic ethnic groups, White and Hispanic participants, who possessed strong positive identities towards their own ethnic group, exhibited higher levels of negative views towards people not belonging to their ethnic group. However, Huddy & Virtanen (1995) propose that people may actually discriminate more among people belonging to their own group, and this assertion is increasingly apparent among Hispanic Americans (McGinley et al., 2010).

## Hispanic sub-groups & Ethnocentrism

Hispanics are one of the largest minority groups in the United States, with ancestral origins that can be traced to approximately 20 different countries, each with their own individual culture (Huddy & Virtanen, 1995; Schwartz & Zamboanga, 2008). Therefore, variations in social and ethnic identity development can often be observed among Hispanic Americans. While these differences are typically noticeable and acknowledged within the overall Hispanic ethnic group, they are oftentimes overlooked by Non-Hispanic individuals (Barlow et al., 2000; Huddy & Virtanen, 1995; Schwartz & Zamboanga, 2008). Still, it is important for these differences to be acknowledged not only by the Hispanic subgroup alone, but also by society as a whole.

Social identity is multifaceted. Cross-cultural researchers have recently been exploring the complexity of ethnic diverse group's social identity, which is often comprised of identification from multiple cultural groups creating multiple social identities rather than just one (Kiang et al., 2008).

For example, one Hispanic American Baptist may equally identify with his/her American culture, as well as with his/her Hispanic culture, and religious affiliation. On the other hand, another Hispanic American Baptist may only identify with his/her American culture and the Catholic culture of his/her spouse.

Prior research indicates that the term Hispanic encompasses too many cultures and should not be examined as one group. A person's beliefs will vary according to their host culture and is often based on a family's level of acculturation (Kane, 2000). A general assumption that all Hispanics share cultural beliefs can create expectations of how all Hispanics should behave, as well as how they should be treated, and can cause stress for Hispanics who do not identify with the expected identity from both Non-Hispanics as well as expectations from other Hispanics (Linton, 2004; Park-Taylor, 2008; Schwartz & Zamboanga, 2008). Cultural variations and acculturative stress can lead to conflict and discrimination among people within the Hispanic ethnic group. This conflict may be due in part to a person's level of ethnocentrism, which can be defined as the level by which a person perceives his/her ethnic group to be superior to another's (Perreault & Bourhis, 1999). Because the Hispanic group can be divided into a variety of ethnic subgroups, e.g. Mexican, Spaniard, Puerto Rican, Columbian, etc., this type of ethnocentrism would be contingent on the ethnic subgroup with which each individual identifies most strongly.

## Hypothesis

Through the utilization of the General Ethnocentrism Scale (Neuliep & McCroskey, 1997) and a self-derived Ethnic Identification and Expectations Scale, this research aimed to clarify that not all Hispanics possess common cultural attitudes and/or customs, simply based on their racial and ethnic status. The purpose of this study was to explore the variations of social identity within the Hispanic ethnic group, by examining the influence of identity on cultural and social expectations, to determine if a relationship existed between these expectations and the racial tension within the Hispanic ethnic group. For the purpose of this study, social identity was defined as the construction of a person's attributes, attitudes, and values, in relation to culture. The term culture, as used in this study, was used to describe learned norms, values, symbols, and language, shared by a group of people, which shapes attitude and behavior.

This study hypothesized that $H_1$: A Hispanic's social identity would influence expectations of which culture other Hispanics "should" identify with, which would lead to prejudices within the Hispanic ethnic group.

# Chapter II

## Method

*Participants*

Participants were recruited through word of mouth from colleagues, fellow students, family, and friends. The snowball sample of participants was comprised of 30 males and 70 females, with a mean age of 32 years, all of Hispanic descent. All participants were able to read and write English.

*Materials*

Each participant completed two scales; a self-developed Ethnic Identification and Expectations questionnaire, used to assess individual levels of Hispanic ethnic identification and expectations, and the Generalized Ethnocentrism scale (alpha=.80$\leq$.90) (Neuliep & McCroskey, 1997).

*Procedure*

90 participants met at a home location in 3 groups of 30 participants each. An additional 20 participants were randomly selected from a computer lab at the University of Texas of the Permian Basin. 10 participants dropped out of the study before submitting their surveys. Data collected from the remaining 100 participants were utilized. After each participant signed a consent form, they were asked to complete a three part Ethnic Identification and Expectations questionnaire and the Generalized Ethnocentrism Scale, in no particular order. Part one of the Ethnic Identification and Expectations questionnaire consisted of basic demographical information regarding gender, age, annual household income, level of education, religious affiliation,

personal country of origin, and familial country of origin. Part two of the survey assessed ancestral background, cultural attitudes, and personal attitudes regarding common racial tensions within the Hispanic culture. The third section of the questionnaire evaluated participant's agreement or disagreement with stereotypical expectations of Hispanic social identity. Upon completion of all questionnaires, participants were debriefed.

All data were then coded. The Ethnic Identification and Expectations questionnaire was comprised of three subscales, which resulted in three scores that were each based on a calculated sum of individual indicators: an identification score (IDS), an expectation score (ES), a racist tendencies score (RTS). Identification Scores ranged from 21-84, based on a calculated sum of 21 variables from a Likert scale (1 = strongly disagree; 2 = disagree; 3 = agree; 4 = strongly agree), whereas the higher the score, the higher the identification with participants' self-identified Hispanic culture. ESs ranged from 18 to 72, and highlighted respondents' attitudes toward Hispanic cultural identity. The ES was based on a calculated sum of 18 expectation indicators, whereas the higher the score, the higher the expectations that other Hispanics should behave according to the customs of their Hispanic origin. In order to assess prejudicial attitudes towards other Hispanics, participant's RTSs had a possible range of 10-40, based on a calculated sum of 10 prejudicial indicators, e.g. using racial slurs to describe Hispanics, whereas higher scores indicate higher levels of racist tendencies towards other Hispanics.

Generalized Ethnocentrism Scores were assessed lastly and were based on a Likert Scale (1=Strongly Disagree; 2= Disagree; 3= Neutral; 4=Agree; 5=Strongly Agree); higher scores were indicative of higher levels of ethnocentrism.

# Chapter III

## Results

Through utilization of a frequency distribution (refer to Table 1, p. 73), it was determined that 74% of the participants (N=100) were of Mexican descent, 12 % were Spaniard, 2% were Puerto Rican, and 12% were of both Mexican and Spanish descent. In terms of religious affiliation, 55% were Catholic, 19 % were Protestant, and 26% identified themselves as nonreligious. Language was a particular point of interest and a frequency distribution indicated that of all participants, 40% were raised in a home where English was the primary language and 66% reported that English is currently the primary language spoken in their home. Moreover, while 7% of the respondents reported an inability to understand or speak Spanish, 15% understand some Spanish but do not know how to speak it, 34% understand and speak Spanish with some difficulty, and 44% understand and speak Spanish with no difficulty, as much as 74% still identified themselves as bilingual.

IDS, ES, RTS, and GES s were analyzed with a variety of variables. Results from a one-way analysis of variance (ANOVA) revealed a significant difference between participants' IDS and the current language spoken in their home ($F(3,96) = 18.596$, $p < .001$), participants' ES and primary language spoken in their home ($F(3,96) = 4.459$, $p < .05$) (refer to Table 2, p. 74).

This study hypothesized that a Hispanic individual's social identity would influence expectations of which culture other Hispanics "should" identify with, which would lead to prejudices within the Hispanic ethnic group. In order to examine the relationship between a Hispanics personal and social identity, with their expectations and biases towards other Hispanics and common Hispanic stereotypes, correlational data was analyzed. Results from a Pearson Correlation supported the hypothesis, resulting in a correlation between a participants' IDS and ES ($r(98) = .634$, $p < .001$), which indicated that participants who identified more closely with their Hispanic culture had higher expectations for other Hispanics to act according to their cultural identification. In addition, a correlation between respondents' IDS and RTS ($r(98) = -451$, $p < .001$) indicated that participants who identified more strongly with their U.S. culture tended to report higher levels of racist tendencies towards other Hispanics (refer to Table 4, p. 76).

An ANOVA was utilized in order to determine the effects of U.S. generational level on a person's identity and expectations. Results from the ANOVA indicated a significant difference between generational level in the U.S. and participants' IDS ($F(4, 95) = 4.887$, $p < .001$) and their ES ($F(4,95) = 4.411$, $p < .05$), but not between generational level and RTS ($F(4, 95) = 1.495$, n.s.) or GES ($F(4, 95) = 1.048$, n.s.) (refer to Table 3, p.75). Similarly, correlational data indicated that as respondents generational level increased their identification with their Hispanic heritage ($r(98) = -.388$, $p < .001$), as well as their expectations for other Hispanics ($r(98) = -.330$, $p < .001$), decreased (refer to Table 4, p. 76).

When examining the relationship between participants' IDS, ES, RTS, and GES, results from a

Pearson Correlation revealed a correlation between respondents' ES and GES (r(98) = 251, p < .05), as well as with their RTS and GES (r(98) = .346, p < .001), suggesting that participants who had higher expectations, and who expressed higher levels of racist tendencies, also demonstrated higher levels of ethnocentrism (refer to Table 5, p. 77). Gender also seemed to factor into a person's RTS (r(98) = .229, p < .05), and GES (r(98) = .189), whereas men expressed higher levels of prejudices towards other Hispanics as well higher levels of ethnocentrism. In addition, in terms of Hispanic origin, results from a t-test indicated a significant difference between participants of Mexican origin and IDS (t(99) = 56.214, p < .001), ES (t(99) = 55.790, p < .001), RTS (t(99) = 39.430, p < .001), GES (t(99) = 41.080, p < .001) in comparison to non-Mexicans. Similarly when examining the relationship between Mexicans vs Non-Mexicans and ES, a correlation revealed that participants of Mexican origin had higher expectations for other Hispanics to act according to the customs of their Hispanic Heritage ($r(98) = -336$, $p < .001$) (refer to Table 4, p. 76), and a one-way ANOVA revealed a significant difference between Hispanic origin and both the IDS ($F(3,96) = 6.795$, $p < .001$) and ES ($F(3,96) = 8.525$, $p < .001$).

Table 1

Frequency Distribution of Origin, Religious Affiliation, and Language.

| Variable | % in Category |
|---|---|
| Gender | |
|     Female | 70% |
|     Male | 30% |
| Hispanic Origin | |
|     Mexican | 74% |
|     Spaniard | 12% |
|     Puerto Rican | 2% |
|     Both Mexican & Spaniard | 12% |
| Religious Affiliation | |
|     Catholic | 55% |
|     Protestant | 19% |
|     Non-Religious | 26% |
| Level of Spanish Fluency | |
|     Do Not Understand or Speak | 7% |
|     Understand but do not Speak | 15% |
|     Understand and Speak with Some Difficulty | 34% |
|     Understand and Speak with No Difficulty | 44% |
| Primary Language Spoken in Childhood Home | |
|     English | 40% |
|     Spanish | 53% |
|     English and Spanish Equally | 7% |
| Primary Language Currently Spoken in Home | |
|     English | 66% |
|     Spanish | 24% |
|     English and Spanish Equally | 10% |

Table 2

Analysis of Variance for Language Currently Spoken in Home and IDS, ES, RTS, & GES.

| Variable Language | Post Hoc Mean Comparison | F-Ratio |
|---|---|---|
| Identification Score | | 18.596** |
| English | -9.477** | |
| English vs Bilingual | 9.477** | |
| Spanish vs. Bilingual | 11.811** | |
| Expectations Score | -3.962* | 4.459* |
| English | 3.962* | |
| English vs Bilingual | 4.420 | |
| Spanish vs. Bilingual | | |
| Racist Tendencies Score | 1.731 | 2.893 |
| English | -1.731 | |
| English vs Bilingual | -4.106 | |
| Spanish vs. Bilingual | | |
| Generalized Ethnocentrism Score | 2.062 | .937 |
| | -2.062 | |
| English | -1.687 | |
| English vs Bilingual | | |
| Spanish vs. Bilingual | | |

*Note.* IDS, ES, and RTS were based on a calculated sum of variables on a Likert scale, from the Ethnic Identification and Expectations questionnaire, where 1=Strongly Disagree, 2=Disagree, 3=Agree, and 4=Strongly Agree. GES was based on a calculated sum of variables on a Likert scale, from a General Ethnocentrism Scale, whereas 1=Strongly Disagree, 2=Disagree, 3=Neutral, 4=Agree, and 5= Strongly Agree.

*p<.05. **p<.001.

Table 3

Analysis of Variance for Generational Level and IDS, ES, RTS, & GES.

| Variable | Df | Mean | F-Ratio |
|---|---|---|---|
| Identification Score | | | |
| Between Groups | 4 | 18.400 | 4.887** |
| Within Groups | 95 | 8.323 | |
| Total | 99 | | |
| Expectations Score | | | |
| Between Groups | 4 | 12.818 | 4.411* |
| Within Groups | 95 | 6.103 | |
| Total | 99 | | |
| Racist Tendencies Score | 4 | 6.192 | 1.459 |
| Between Groups | 95 | 5.126 | |
| Within Groups | 99 | | |
| Total | | | |
| GES | | | |
| Between Groups | 4 | 6.803 | 1.048 |
| Within Groups | 95 | 6.646 | |
| Total | 99 | | |

*Note.* IDS, ES, and RTS were based on a calculated sum of variables on a Likert scale, from the Ethnic Identification and Expectations questionnaire, where 1=Strongly Disagree, 2=Disagree, 3=Agree, and 4=Strongly Agree. GES was based on a calculated sum of variables on a Likert scale, from a General Ethnocentrism Scale, whereas 1=Strongly Disagree, 2=Disagree, 3=Neutral, 4=Agree, and 5= Strongly Agree.

*$p<.05$. **$p<.001$.

Table 4

Correlational Data between Generational Level, Hispanic Origin, and IDS, ES, RTS, and GES.

| Variable | IDS | ES | RTS | GES |
|---|---|---|---|---|
| U.S. Generational Level | -.388** | -.330** | .193 | .093 |
| Hispanic Origin | -.188 | -.336** | .008 | .066 |

*Note.* IDS, ES, and RTS were based on a calculated sum of variables on a Likert scale, from the Ethnic Identification and Expectations questionnaire, where 1=Strongly Disagree, 2=Disagree, 3=Agree, and 4=Strongly Agree. GES was based on a calculated sum of variables on a Likert scale, from a General Ethnocentrism Scale, whereas 1=Strongly Disagree, 2=Disagree, 3=Neutral, 4=Agree, and 5= Strongly Agree. Hispanic Origin was divided into two groups for this comparison, participants of Mexican origin and Non-Mexican participants.

*p<.05. **p<.001.

Table 5

Correlational Data for IDS, ES, RTS, and GES.

| Variable | ES | RTS | General Ethnocentrism Score (GES) |
|---|---|---|---|
| Identification Score (IDS) | .634** | .451** | -.111 |
| Expectations Score (ES) | ----- | -.048 | .251* |
| Racist Tendencies Score (RTS) | ----- | ----- | .346** |

*Note.* IDS, ES, and RTS were based on a calculated sum of variables on a Likert scale, from the Ethnic Identification and Expectations questionnaire, where 1=Strongly Disagree, 2=Disagree, 3=Agree, and 4=Strongly Agree. GES was based on a calculated sum of variables on a Likert scale, from a General Ethnocentrism Scale, whereas 1=Strongly Disagree, 2=Disagree, 3=Neutral, 4=Agree, and 5= Strongly Agree.

*p<.05. **p<.001.

Table 1B
Mean and Standard Deviation for IDS Variables

| Variable | Strongly Agree/ Always | Agree /Some | Disagree /Rarely | Strongly Disagree/ Never | Mean | s.d. |
|---|---|---|---|---|---|---|
| English* | 90 | 8 | ---- | 2 | 1.14 | .493 |
| Spanish | 30 | 39 | 20 | 11 | 2.88 | .967 |
| Bilingual | ---- | 74 | 26 | ---- | 1.74 | .441 |
| English current language | 66 | 8 | ---- | 26 | 1.52 | .882 |
| Holidays of Hispanic Heritage | 18 | 30 | 31 | 21 | 2.45 | 1.019 |
| US Holidays* | 45 | 38 | 11 | 6 | 1.78 | .871 |
| Proud of American Heritage* | 46 | 49 | 1 | 4 | 1.63 | .706 |
| Proud of Hispanic Heritage | 46 | 49 | 2 | 3 | 3.38 | .678 |
| Don't mind Latino | 25 | 56 | 13 | 6 | 3.00 | .791 |
| Don't mind Chicano | 14 | 46 | 27 | 13 | 2.61 | .886 |
| Don't mind Mexican American | 28 | 53 | 7 | 12 | 2.97 | .915 |
| Don't mind Hispanic | 34 | 59 | 6 | 1 | 3.26 | .613 |
| Rather be called American* | 22 | 22 | 46 | 10 | 2.44 | .946 |
| Don't mind White* | 11 | 22 | 37 | 30 | 2.86 | .975 |
| Identify more closely with Hispanic | 8 | 18 | 56 | 18 | 2.16 | .813 |

| | | | | | | |
|---|---|---|---|---|---|---|
| Bothered When Clerk Switches* from English to Spanish | 13 | 19 | 46 | 22 | 2.77 | .941 |
| Shouldn't have to learn Spanish* | 12 | 18 | 40 | 30 | 2.88 | .977 |
| Offended when people assume I don't speak English* | 21 | 33 | 34 | 12 | 2.37 | .950 |
| Born in US are American regardless of Ethnicity* | 45 | 37 | 16 | 2 | 1.75 | .796 |

*Note.* IDS based on a calculated sum of variables on a Likert scale, from the Ethnic Identification and Expectations questionnaire, whereas 1=Strongly Disagree, 2=Disagree, 3=Agree, and 4=Strongly Agree.

*Reversed Scored Variables.

Table 2B
Mean and Standard Deviation of ES Variables

| Variable | Strongly Agree | Agree | Disagree | Strongly Disagree | Mean | s.d. |
|---|---|---|---|---|---|---|
| Assume all Hispanics speak Spanish | 4 | 14 | 58 | 24 | 1.98 | .738 |
| All Hispanics Should Speak Spanish | 17 | 33 | 33 | 17 | 2.50 | .969 |
| Refer to Hispanics as Mexicans | 4 | 38 | 33 | 25 | 2.21 | .868 |
| U.S. Hispanics should know more about U.S. Heritage than Hispanic Heritage* | 7 | 26 | 41 | 26 | 2.86 | .888 |
| Proper English | 3 | 5 | 40 | 52 | 1.59 | .726 |
| No reason that particular Hispanic should speak Spanish* | 11 | 30 | 44 | 15 | 2.63 | .872 |
| Hispanics should learn English in U.S.* | 32 | 45 | 18 | 5 | 1.96 | .840 |
| Hispanics should know how to speak Spanish | 15 | 33 | 42 | 10 | 2.53 | .870 |
| Hispanics should be Proud of Heritage | 14 | 41 | 35 | 10 | 2.38 | .749 |
| Hispanics should be more Americanized* | 6 | 14 | 67 | 13 | 2.87 | .706 |

| | | | | | | |
|---|---|---|---|---|---|---|
| Hispanics share same culture | 1 | 8 | 60 | 31 | 1.79 | .624 |
| Hispanic Pride Openly | 3 | 45 | 39 | 13 | 2.59 | .854 |
| Same family values | 3 | 1 | 61 | 35 | 1.72 | .637 |
| No different than U.S. Whites and Blacks* | 31 | 45 | 19 | 5 | 1.98 | .841 |
| No Hispanic Pride | 2 | 5 | 56 | 37 | 1.72 | .653 |
| Doesn't Speak Spanish wants to be White | 2 | 3 | 49 | 46 | 1.61 | .650 |
| No Spanish Music Ashamed | 2 | 4 | 41 | 53 | 1.55 | .672 |
| Talk White | 1 | 3 | 48 | 48 | 1.57 | .607 |

*Note.* ES based on a calculated sum of variables on a Likert scale, from the Ethnic Identification and Expectations questionnaire, whereas 1=Strongly Disagree, 2=Disagree, 3=Agree, and 4=Strongly Agree.

*Reversed Scored Variables.

Table 3B
Mean and Standard Deviation of RTS variables

| Variable | Strongly Agree | Agree | Disagree | Strong/ Disagree | Mean | s.d. |
|---|---|---|---|---|---|---|
| American Hispanics Smarter | 4 | 9 | 44 | 43 | 1.74 | .787 |
| Offended if referred to as other Hispanic | 11 | 16 | 43 | 30 | 2.08 | .950 |
| Called someone coconut | 13 | 27 | 14 | 46 | 2.07 | 1.121 |
| Called someone a wet-back | 14 | 39 | 19 | 28 | 2.39 | 1.043 |
| Okay to use racist terms | 6 | 28 | 44 | 22 | 2.18 | .845 |
| Used racist terms to describe other Hispanics | 15 | 38 | 21 | 26 | 2.42 | 1.037 |
| All Hispanic Men are Domineering | 3 | 15 | 60 | 22 | 1.99 | .703 |
| Better than other Hispanics | 6 | 6 | 41 | 47 | 1.71 | .832 |
| Other Hispanics Give Me a Bad Name | 9 | 22 | 44 | 25 | 2.15 | .903 |
| Racist against other Hispanics | 4 | 13 | 29 | 54 | 1.67 | .853 |

*Note.* RTS based on a calculated sum of variables on a Likert scale, from the Ethnic Identification and Expectations questionnaire, whereas 1=Strongly Disagree, 2=Disagree, 3=Agree, and 4=Strongly Agree.

Table 4B

Percent Level of Agreement of Common Labels and Stereotypes

| Variable | Agree | Disagree |
|---|---|---|
| Been Called Racist Terms by Other Hispanics | 57% | 43% |
| Been Called Coconut | 30% | 70% |
| Been Called Wet-Back | 50% | 50% |
| Other Hispanics Give Me a Bad Name | 31% | 69% |
| Racist Against Other Hispanics | 17% | 83% |
| Better Than Other Hispanics | 12% | 88% |
| Offended if Referred to As Wrong Hispanic Origin | 27% | 73% |
| Don't Mind Being Called Latino | 81% | 19% |
| Don't Mind Being Called Chicano | 60% | 40% |
| Don't Mind Being Called Hispanic | 92% | 8% |
| Don't Mind Being Called Mexican-American | 81% | 19% |
| Don't Mind Being Called White | 33% | 67% |
| Rather Be Called American | 44% | 56% |
| There Are Cultural Differences Between Hispanics | 85% | 15% |
| U.S. Born Hispanics are no Different than U.S. Born Whites or Blacks | 76% | 24% |

Chapter IV

Discussion

The purpose of this study was to explore the differences among personal cultural identification, social identification, and expectations within the Hispanic ethnic group, in order to examine the socio-cultural implications of the cultural expectations of Hispanic humans in the United States, in hopes to bring awareness to the impact that racial division, human division based on skin tone, has negatively affected humans...to the extent that even humans classified as the same racial and/or ethnic groups, will discriminate against one another.

Prior research has indicated that racially based assumptions can be detrimental to therapeutic success (Gurung & Mehta, 2001) primarily because most people would rather be judged on characteristics that they have control over, e.g. likes, dislikes, morals, and/or values, rather than on ascribed attributes that they have no control over, e.g. race/ethnicity, skin tone, and/or place of birth (Markus, 2008; Negy et al., 2003). The primary reason for this study was to highlight different attitudes among Hispanics in order to help future clinicians avoid misdiagnosis of Hispanic clients, which can occur when a clinician makes assumptions that a client's presenting problems are culturally bias, without first identifying the client's self-proclaimed cultural identity.

For example, there are many possible cultural differences between a 6$^{th}$ generation U.S. born Hispanic female, who is raised in an English speaking Protestant home, and a 1$^{st}$ generation U.S.

born Hispanic female, raised in a Spanish speaking Catholic home.

This study hypothesized that a Hispanic individual's social identity would influence expectations of which culture other Hispanics "should" identify with, which would lead to prejudices within the Hispanic ethnic group. Each participant completed two scales; a self-developed Ethnic Identification and Expectations questionnaire, used to assess individual levels of Hispanic ethnic identification and expectations, and the Generalized Ethnocentrism scale, which was developed by Neuliep & McCroskey (1997). There were a total of 110 Hispanic participants. During administration, 4 participants withdrew from the study, and 6 more refused to submit their survey upon completion. Data from the remaining participants (N=100) was analyzed. Results from an ANOVA and Pearson Correlation, supported the hypothesis.

The Ethnocentrism and Identification questionnaire was comprised of three subscales: identification (IDS), expectation (ES), and racists tendencies (RTS). Each subscale was based on a calculated sum of variables (21 for the IDS, 18 for the ES, and 10 for the RTS), whereas the higher the score on the IDS and ES the higher the level of identification with and expectations for other Hispanics to identify with their Hispanic heritage, versus their American culture, and higher RTS scores indicated higher racist tendencies towards other Hispanics. In terms of IDS indicators, results demonstrated that while 26% felt stronger identification with the customs of the country of their Hispanic origin than with that of the U.S., 95% were proud of their American Heritage, and 44% would rather be referred to Americans than any other listed "Hispanic" identifier (e.g. Latino, Chicano, Mexican-American, and Hispanic). For a list of IDS variables, including a tally of responses along with the mean and standard deviation of each indicator, refer to Table 1B, p. 78).

ES variables included questions regarding what participants thought other Hispanics 'should' or 'shouldn't' do (refer to Table 2B, p. 80). 91% of the participants indicated that they do not believe Hispanics share the same culture, and although 95% of the participants claim to be proud of their Hispanic heritage, only 55% expected other Hispanics to feel the same, 20% felt other Hispanics should be more Americanized, and 76% believed that other U.S. born Hispanics should not be expected to be any different than U.S. born Non-Hispanic Whites or Blacks. In general, correlation results indicated that Hispanics with high IDSs also had high ESs ($r(98) = .634$, $p < .001$), suggesting that people who identified more strongly with U.S. culture expected other Hispanics to be more Americanized, and vice versa (refer to Table 5, p. 77).

The current study was considered controversial and the RTS was comprised of some of the most controversial variables, and some of the most contradictory results. For example, only 17% of the participants admitted to being racist towards other Hispanics, even though 43% reported that they have used racist terms to describe other Hispanics, which is low considering that 53% have called other Hispanics wet-backs and 40% have called another Hispanic a coconut. Similarly, 21% said other Hispanics give them a bad name and 27% reported that they would be offended if they were referred to as the wrong Hispanic origin, for example being called a Mexican when they were actually Spaniard, Puerto Rican, Cuban, etc., which lead to a particular area of interest, Hispanic labels.

This study was interested in exploring common stereotypic expectations and found, as expected, a variety of disagreement across variables. In fact, many participants could not even agree as to what term they preferred to be called, e.g. Chicano, Latino, Mexican-American, Hispanic, American, or White (refer to Table 4B, p. 83). There is no question that minorities struggle with inconsistencies between their personal identification and the perceived identification from others.

For example, a Hispanic college student whose Non-Hispanic academic advisor suggests majoring in Spanish, without knowing whether or not the student speaks Spanish; or, the Hispanic clerk who addresses a non-Spanish speaking Hispanic, in Spanish, because he/she assumes that all Hispanics speak Spanish, just because he/she does. During debriefing, one participant stated, "Hispanics are the only Whites, and sometimes Blacks, that are expected to identify their specific ethnicity. If you are German, Irish, Italian, etc., you are just called White. But not even Spanish 'Hispanics' can say that. We're singled out, and half the time we don't even know what to call ourselves. Well if I don't even know, how do you?"

As previously mentioned, 10 participants dropped out of the study. Moreover, during the debriefing, many participants expressed that the questions were upsetting because it made them question the reasoning behind their beliefs. Still, almost every participant stated that they wish every Hispanic could take the survey, which leads to one of the major disadvantages of this study.

This study focused only on Hispanics from the Permian Basin. It would be beneficial for future research to collect data from a larger geographic region, and although the sample was demographically diverse, a snowball sample, while convenient, was not ideal. In addition, the current study relied on two separate questionnaires; a self-derived Ethnic Identification and Expectations questionnaire and the Generalized Ethnocentrism Scale (Neuliep & McCroskey, 1997). Questionnaires were given in no particular order, in order to avoid order effect on the results. However, there were a total of 107 questions. It is undetermined as to whether or not the length of the questionnaires affected participant's responses. Future research may need to make adjustments, in order to avoid response fatigue. In addition, as previously mentioned, the main instrument utilized in this study was self-derived and although correlational data lends partial support to the validity of the Identification and Expectations Questionnaire (refer to Table 5, p. 77), further inter-item analysis and comparisons to similar tests would be beneficial in the standardization of this particular instrument, for future use.

This study aimed to uncover the differences within Hispanics, in order to help clinicians understand that a Hispanic client should not be expected to follow a general rule of thumb that is based solely on their assigned ethnic label. Instead, the clinician should take the client's personal identification and experiences into account. As demonstrated in this sample, not all Hispanics shared the same attitudes. Overall, research on the socio-cultural implications of Hispanic social identity is limited, and further research is highly recommended. It should also be noted that while this study was a study for the field of psychology, results may be beneficial to other disciplines such as, sociology, cultural studies, education, demographical data collection, etc. The current study focused on the Hispanic subculture. However, it is my hope to expand the study to encompass all races, in order to study my initial speculation, that there are more differences within ethnic groups than there are between them, in order to explore the possibility that race is an illusion created to fuel inequality.

Humans

References

Barlow, K.M., Taylor, D. M., & Lambert, W. (2000). Ethnicity in America and feeling "American". *The Journal of Psychology, 134*, 581-600.

Basow, S.A., Lilley, E., Bookwala, J., & McGillicuddy-DeLisi, A. (2008). Identity development and psychological well-being in Korean-born adoptees in the U.S. *American Journal of Orthopsychiatry, 78*, 473-480.

Branscombe, N.R., & Wann, D.L. (1994). Collective self-esteem consequences of outgroup derogation when a valued social identity is on trial. *European Journal of Social Pyschology, 24*, 641-657.

De Cremer, D. (2001). Relations of self-esteem concerns, group identification, and self-stereotyping to in-group favoritism. *The Journal of Social Psychology, 141*, 389-400.

DeCremer, D., VanVugt, M., & Sharp, J. (1999). Effects of collective self-esteem on ingroup evaluations. *The Journal of Social Psychology, 139*, 530-532,

Ethier, K.A., & Deaux, K. (1994). Negotiating social identity when contexts change: Maintaining identification and responding to threat. *Journal of Personality and Social Psychology, 67*, 243-251.

Ford, G.C. (2006). Ethical reasoning for mental health professionals. Thousand Oaks, CA: Sage Publications, Inc.

Gurung, R.A.R., & Mehta, V. (2001). Relating ethnic identity, acculturation, and attitudes toward treating minority clients. *Cultural Diversity and Ethnic Minority Psychology, 7*, 139-151.

Huddy, L., & Virtanen, S. (1995). Subgroup differentiation and subgroup bias among Latinos as a function of familiarity and positive distinctiveness. *Journal of Personality and Social Psychology, 68*, 97-108.

Kane, Emily W. (2000). Racial and ethnic variations in gender-related attitudes. *Annual Review of Sociology, 26*, 419-439.

Kiang, L., Yip, T., & Fuligni, A.J. (2008). Multiple social identities and adjustment in young adults from ethnically diverse backgrounds. *Journal of Research on Adolescence, 18*, 643-670.

Linton, A. (2004). A critical mass model of bilingualism among U.S.-born Hispanics. *Social Forces, 83*, 279-314.

Markus, H.R. (2008). Pride, prejudice, and ambivalence: Toward a unified theory of race and ethnicity. *American Psychologist, 63*, 651-665

McGinley, M., Carlo, G., Crockett, L.J., Raffaelli, M., Stone, R.A., & Iturbide, M.I. (2010). Stressed and helping: The relations among acculturative stress, gender, and prosocial tendencies in Mexican Americans. *The Journal of Social Psychology, 150*, 34-56.

Negy, C., Shreve, T.L., Jensen, B.J., & Uddin, N. (2003). Ethnic identity, self-esteem, and ethnocentrism: A study of social identity versus multicultural theory of development. *Cultural Diversity and Ethnic Minority Psychology, 9*, 333-344.

Neuliep, J.W. & McCroskey, J.C. (1997). The development of a U.S. and Generalized

Ethnocentrism Scale. *Communication Research Reports, 14*, 385-398.

Park-Taylor, J., Ng, V., Ventura, A.B., Kang, A.E., Morris, C.R., Gilbert, T., Srivastava, D., & Androsiglio, R.A. (2008). What it means to be and feel like a "true" American. *Cultural Diversity and Ethnic minority Psychology, 14*, 128-137.

Perreault, S., & Bourhis, R.Y. (1999). Ethnocentrism, social identification, and discrimination. *Personality and Social Psychology Bulletin, 25*, 92-103.

Rotheram-Borus, M.J. (1990). Adolescents' reference-group choices, self-esteem, and adjustment. *Journal of Personality and Social Psychology, 59*, 1075-1081.

Sue, D.W., Arredondo, P., & McDavis, R.J. (1992). Multicultural counseling competencies and standards: A call to the profession. *Journal of Counseling & Development, 70*, 477-484.

Schwartz, S.J., & Zamboanga, B.L. (2008). Testing Berry's model of acculturation. *Cultural Diversity and Ethnic Minority Psychology, 14*, 275-285.

Utsey, S. O., Chae, M. H., Brown, C. F., & Kelly, D. (2002). Effect of ethnic group membership on ethnic identity, race-related stress, and quality of life. *Cultural Diversity and Ethnic Minority Psychology, 8*, 366-377.

White, C.R., O'Brien, K., Jackson, L.J., Havalchak, A., Phillips, C.M., Thomas, P., & Cabrera, J. (2008). Ethnic identity development among adolescents in foster care. *Child Adolescence Social Work Journal, 25*, 497-515.

# "species

*noun* spe·cies \ˈspē-(ˌ)shēz, -(ˌ)sēz\

biology : a group of animals or plants that are similar and can produce young animals or plants : a group of related animals or plants that is smaller than a genus

~

: a particular group of things or people that belong together or have some shared quality"

Species. (n.d.). Retrieved February 5, 2016, from http://www.merriam-webster.com/dictionary/species

# Notes

Humans

# Notes

Humans

# NOTES

Humans

# "Homo sapiens

*noun* Ho·mo sa·pi·ens \ˌhō-(ˌ)mō-ˈsā-pē-ˌenz, -ənz, *especially British* -ˈsa-pē-ənz\

: the **species** of human beings that exist today"

Homo sapiens. (n.d.). Retrieved February 5, 2016, from http://www.merriam-webster.com/dictionary/Homo sapiens

Humans

# Notes

# "Ethnic Group:

a social group or category of the population that, in a larger society, is set apart and bound together by common ties of race, language, nationality, or culture."

ethnic group. (2016). In *Encyclopædia Britannica*. Retrieved from http://www.britannica.com/topic/ethnic-group

# Notes

Humans

# NOTES

Rather than maintaining organizations such as the National Association for the Advancement of Colored People (NAACP).....

why not promote a National Association for the Advancement of All People?

# Notes

Humans

# Notes

# "discriminate

*verb* dis·crim·i·nate \dis-ˈkri-mə-ˌnāt\

*intransitive verb*

**1a :** to make a distinction <*discriminate among historical sources*>
**b :** to use good judgment

~

**2 :** to make a difference in treatment or favor on a basis other than individual merit"

Discriminate (n.d.). Retrieved February 5, 2016, from http://www.merriam-webster.com/dictionary/Discriminate

# NOTES

Humans

# Eliminate racial labels

from

everyday speech…..

Humans

# Notes

# Humans

# Notes

- ✓ You are all human.
- ✓ You all have the same basic needs.
- ✓ You all have to share this earth…

…so now what?

Humans

Made in the USA
San Bernardino, CA
30 March 2016